NEWLYN
A Brief History

by

Margaret E. Perry

Illustrations by Jeffrey E. Lawrence

Cover picture: Jeffrey E. Lawrence

Published by Margaret E. Perry, 24 Charles Street, Newlyn, Penzance
Cornwall TR18 5QB
Printed by Headland Printers Ltd., Bread Street, Penzance, Cornwall

ISBN 0 9534356 1 X

Acknowledgements

Thanks are due to Ben Batten for permission to use the extract from his book *Newlyn Towners, Fishermen and Methodists*. The frontispiece is after a water-colour *Old Tolcarne Bridge, Newlyn* painted by H.P.Tremenheere in 1804, now in private ownership. Thanks also go to Molly Goriely for reading and commenting on the text, and for assistance in proof reading.

Copyright - Text: Margaret E. Perry 1999
Copyright - Illustrations: Jeffrey E. Lawrence 1999

No part of this publication may be reproduced, stored in a retrieval system, or transmitted in any form or by any means, electronic, mechanical, photocopying, recording or otherwise without the prior permission of the copyright owner.

1278	First recorded use of name of Newlyn.
1302	Tolcarne first mentioned in records.
1337	Duchy of Cornwall formed.
1437	Indulgence granted to those assisting in the repair of a quay at Newlyn.
1595	Village burned by Spaniards.
1623	Court action to compel use of Manorial mill at Tolcarne brought against inhabitants of parish.
1680	Newlyn fishermen sued for non-payment of tithes.
1714	Final case against Corporation of Penzance to enforce Manorial rights at Tolcarne Mill.
1725	New tithe crisis: 118 fishermen sued.
1738	Storms severely damage Newlyn quay.
1747	John Wesley first visits Newlyn.
1789	Wesley's fourteenth and last visit.
1800	William Lovett, Social Reformer, born in Newlyn.
1826	Boats start going to Ireland for herring fishery.
1828	Wheal Henry mine shaft sunk.
1832	Trinity Wesleyan Methodist Church built. Cholera outbreak in Newlyn.
1835	Ebenezer Primitive Methodist Church built.
1848	Ecclesiastical parish of Newlyn formed.
1854	*Mystery* sails to Australia.
1866	Parish church built, dedicated to St. Peter.
1880	Severe storm destroys road to Penzance.
1883	New Road and road bridge built.
1885	Foundation stone of South Pier laid.
1886	27 artists recorded as living in Newlyn.
1890	Newlyn Industrial Class founded. Penlee Quarry first worked.
1894	North Pier completed.
1895	Newlyn Art Gallery opens.
1896	Newlyn men riot over Sunday fishing.
1908	Strand joins Street-an-Nowan and 'Newlyn Town'
1911	RNMDSF Ship Institute opened.
1927	Centenary Primitive Methodist Chapel built.
1934	Newlyn becomes part of Borough of Penzance.
1937	*Rosebud* sails to London with petition.
1980	Mary Williams pier completed.

Old Tolcarne Bridge, Newlyn

NEWLYN IN PENWITH

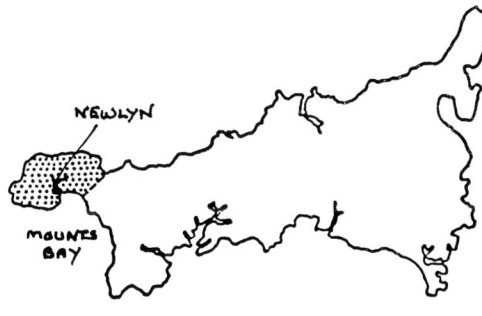

Newlyn has an interesting geographical location. Situated on the shores of Mounts Bay to the south of the range of granite hills which form the backbone of the Penwith peninsula, the scenery is in sharp contrast to that of the high rocky cliffs and inaccessible shoreline of the north coast of Cornwall.
In the lower part of the village between the Newlyn and Lariggan rivers,[1] the land slopes gradually to the shore. Between Newlyn and Mousehole the road runs along what geologists have described as a 'raised-beach platform' caused by the lowering of the sea level during an interglacial period some 20,000 years ago. This platform has been constantly eroded over the centuries; in the villages retaining walls have been built, forming a defence against the encroachment of the sea. From here the cliffs to Lands End are lower than on the north coast and there are no cliffs between Newlyn and Marazion.

The village as we know it today has evolved from a number of small hamlets. Tolcarne, to the north of the Newlyn river, mainly an industrial area until the late nineteenth century, was part of the parish of Madron until 1848, when the ecclesiastical parish of Newlyn St. Peter was formed. Street-an-Nowan lies to the south of the river and includes the area known as the Fradgan. This 'Street-an-Nowan' is believed to derive from the Cornish *Stret an oghen,* street of the oxen, or ox-way, and 'Fradgan' has the same meaning from *forth oghen,* ox road.[2] Newlyn 'town' on the cliff at the top of the hill evolved as a fishing community, its houses clustered around the medieval quay. As the village grew and linked

5

these three areas it also absorbed farming communities including Trewarveneth, Chywoone and Gwavas. The name 'Newlyn' is probably of English origin from the word *lyn*, pool. Possibly it is used here to denote a sheltered anchorage. The first recorded use of the name was in 1278 and it refers to the deep-water anchorage between Newlyn and Mousehole known as Gwavas lake, sheltered from the prevailing west and south-west winds. In the 16th century Leland wrote

.......also in the bay is a good road for ships called Gwavas Lake.[3]

Tolcarne and the Buccaboo

Tolcarne, taking its name from the Cornish *tal carn*, brow of a rock-pile, is mentioned in records dating from 1302. The carn today is mainly overgrown and obscured by houses, but in earlier times its rocky heights loomed over the Newlyn river and the wooded coombe. An outcrop of blue elvan (greenstone), the summit has a net-like pattern which features in the story of the buccaboo, or storm devil, from whom Newlyn people take their nickname of *Newlyn buccas*. The story has been told on numerous occasions over the centuries. This account is related in a book entitled *Once in Cornwall:*

> A Newlyn fisherman, after a good night's fishing, spread his nets on the shore to dry. It happened that, as the weather was calm and fine, the storm devil, Buccaboo, was out of a job, and so was strolling rather forlornly on the beach. Presently, he catches sight of the fisherman's nets spread over some bushes. 'Ho, ho!' says he to himself. 'I was unfortunately prevented from stopping his fishing last night, but I can at least make sure that he does not go out tonight, or any other night until he has made a new net.' And, with that, he picks up the nets and flies off with them. The fisherman was just coming through his cottage door to begin mending the broken meshes, when he happens to turn round, and sees the Buccaboo flying off trailing the nets after him.
>
> It just happened to be the time of day when the choir of Paul Church was accustomed to practise, so the fisherman rushed off there and ran up to the priest crying out that the devil had taken his fishing nets and was flying off with them. The priest, fortunately, was a quick man with his wits and in one second he had found a way to defeat the fiend and

his wickedness. You know that there is one thing that no devil can stand the sound of, and that is the Creed; it hurts his pride by reminding him of how all his schemes of vengeance came to nothing. 'Follow me,' cries the priest, beckoning to the choir. 'Sing the Creed as you go, and keep on singing it, every mother's son of you until I give you leave to stop.'

Off went the priest and off went the choir singing lustily; and there was Buccaboo perched on the top of the cliff resting himself, for he found the wet nets a goodly weight to lug after him. As soon as he heard the voices of Paul choir, he gave an awful screech and flew away dragging the nets after him. Off went the choir in pursuit, still singing. Buccaboo flew until his breath was all gone, and then he perched again, on a tree top this time; but he had not been there for many seconds when he heard *'Confiteor unum baptisma in remissionem peccatorum'* coming up the lea of the hill, and with a frightful yell off he set again. He could have outdistanced his pursuers by dropping the nets, but this he was loath to do because such a confession of failure was too big a hurt to his pride. All day long the chase continued; Buccaboo being driven from one place to another, and the choir, though worn out, and breathless, giving him no rest.

At last, when evening came, he made one last effort to escape with the nets by flying over the Coombe to Tolcarne. He hadn't come to rest for many minutes, when he again heard the choir coming over the Coombe, very hoarse and breathless, but still singing the Creed. So, at that he gave in to the better man, and with one last cry of baffled rage, dropped the nets, turning them into stone as he did so, and then disappeared. The stone nets lie there to this very day.[4]

Until quite recent times, Newlyn fishermen had a custom of leaving a few fish on the beach or quay to placate the Buccaboo - one of many superstitions connected with fishing.

The Early Years

One of the earliest references to Newlyn can be found in the annual payments made by fishing ports to the Duchy of Cornwall in the year of its formation, 1337. These payments were based on the number of fishing boats supported by each port. The payment by Newlyn was only ten shillings (50p); this contrasts with £5 paid by Mousehole and £3 by Marazion. Penzance, like Newlyn relatively unimportant at this date, paid twelve shillings (60p).[5] Mousehole, just two miles

along the coast from Newlyn and today a much smaller village, was granted markets and fairs as early as 1292 and the chapel of St. Mary was first licensed there in 1383. By 1500 Penzance, Marazion, Mousehole and St. Ives each had a chapel, quay, markets and fairs. It is known that Newlyn had a quay, as in 1437 the Bishop of Exeter, Edmund Lacy, granted an Indulgence to those assisting in the repair of the quay at Newlyn.[6]

At this time fishermen would have lived and worked in the small cluster of houses around the medieval quay. Beyond, farming was the main occupation and this is reflected in some of the surviving street names of Cornish derivation in the area: *Bowgey*, cow-house *(bugh, chy)* and *Gwavas*, winter dwelling or pasture. As late as 1841 the tithe map for the parish of Paul shows orchards and fields surrounding the small communities of Newlyn and Street-an-Nowan, in some cases stretching down to the shoreline. Leland visiting Newlyn in the early sixteenth century as antiquary to Henry VIII, described the village:

> Newlyn is a poore fisher towne and hath only a key for shippes and bootes with a lytle socur of land water.[7]

The most memorable event of the sixteenth century occured on the 23rd July 1595 when, in the early morning, four Spanish galleys appeared off the coast near Mousehole and landed a raiding party which sacked and burned that village. They destroyed not only the village and surrounding houses but also the parish church of St. Pol de Leon. After firing Mousehole and Paul the Spaniards withdrew but later in the day went ashore at Newlyn and burned this village before continuing to Penzance. A contemporary account of the raid was printed in 1602 in Richard Carew's *Survey of Cornwall*. Carew would have had a firsthand account from his friend Sir Francis Godolphin, who had attempted to muster the local men to offer some resistance to the Spaniards. Apparently with little success. On July 25th, the wind being favourable, the Spaniards departed. There were three fatal casualties of the raid, including one 'James of Newlyn'. The parish registers of Paul having been destroyed in the raid, the burials of these three men form the first entries in the new register.

The Cornish Language

Evidence exists that as early as 1600 the Cornish language was already in decline, although it continued to be spoken in West Penwith (rarely as a first language) until about 1800. John Norden (c.1548-1625) wrote:

> ....In the west part of the country...the Cornish tongue is most in use among the inhabitants, and yet though the husband and wife, parents and children, master and servants, do mutually communicate in their native language, yet there is none of them in manner but is able to converse with a stranger in the English tongue, unless it be some obscure people that seldom confer with the better sort. But it seems that in a few years the Cornish language will be by little and little abandoned.[8]

At least half a century later John Ray, the naturalist, who visited Cornwall in 1662, reported:

> ...Mr Dicken Gwyn [Dick Angwin] was considered as the only person who could then write in the Cornish language; and who lived in one of the most western parishes called St. Just *where there were few* but could speak English; while few of the children could speak Cornish, so that the language would soon be lost.[9]

As vernacular use of the language declined so efforts were being made by a number of Cornish scholars to preserve literary relics and to record as much of the Cornish language as possible. John Keigwin of Mousehole was arguably the greatest scholar among these men, but also prominent were the Boson family of Newlyn, Nicholas, Thomas and John (fl.1660-1730). Their relationship is uncertain but it is likely that Nicholas was John's father, and Thomas a cousin. Nicholas Boson wrote a short essay, both in Cornish and English, called *Nebbaz Gerriau dro tho Carnoack*, 'A Few Words about Cornish', with some folk tales to amuse and instruct his children. The best known of these *Jowan Chy-an-Horth py An Try Foynt a Skyans*, John of Chyanhorth, or 'The Three Maxims', was first printed by Edward Lhuyd, the Celtic philologist, in his *Archaeologia Britannica* in 1707. In this century the story was again to be used as a teaching aid when Robert Morton Nance included it in a text book *Cornish for All*, produced for the Federation of Old Cornwall Societies in 1929. After years of study Nance produced a unified spelling system which greatly facilitated the learning of Cornish. Henry

Jenner had previously in 1904 published his *Handbook of the Cornish Language*. He was a brilliant scholar, active in the Philological Society, and was largely responsible for creating an interest among British scholars in the Cornish language. In 1901 he instigated the formation of *Cowethas Kelto-Kernuak* - the Celtic Cornish Society - the first Cornish language movement.

Among the writings of Thomas and John Boson are some translations of biblical texts, the Ten Commandments, Lord's Prayer and Creed. John Boson also wrote a Pilchard-curing rhyme. Several versions exist with slight variations, one copy has an endorsement in the hand of a contemporary Cornish scholar, John Gwavas: 'verses in the Cornish language to cure pilchards for foreign markets per John Boson of Newlyn in Paul.'[10]

Writing in 1884 the Rev. W. S. Lach-Szyrma, then vicar of St. Peter's Church, Newlyn, stated that a few elderly people in the village, who had learned the numerals in childhood, could still count in Cornish. He also considered that about 200 words were still retained in use at that time from the Cornish language.[11]

Newlyn and the Mounts Bay Fisheries

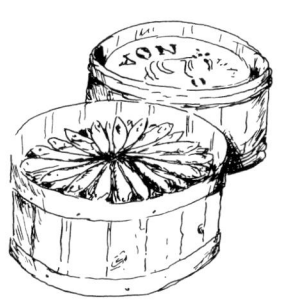

Here's a health to the Pope
And may he repent,
And lengthen six months
The term of his Lent.
It's always declared
Betwixt the two poles
There's nothing like pilchards
For saving of souls.

The parish of Paul was one of the most important fishing parishes in Cornwall in the seventeenth century. The most valuable fish caught by the fishermen of Newlyn was the pilchard, a mature sardine. As well as being consumed locally they were cured and exported, chiefly to France, Italy, Spain and countries bordering on the Mediterranean. Exports of pilchards from Cornwall are recorded as early as the mid sixteenth century. By the mid 1700s, trade was well established and landings of pilchards gradually increased, reaching a peak in 1871. After that date pilchard stocks declined rapidly. Today only one firm, British Cured Pilchards Ltd, based in Newlyn, produces pressed pilchards for export.

Pilchards

After spawning in the Spring at the entrance to the Channel, pilchards approached the land in shoals during the late summer, but their habits were inconsistent. The area and time they appeared could vary from year to year. In the eighteenth century, fishermen from the parish reported taking more pilchards in the winter in the Mounts Bay area. The fish caught during the colder months were larger than those caught in the summer, being fatter and having greater oil content. Pilchard oil was a highly desired commodity, for heating and lighting and in manufacturing trades. The fishy residues were a useful manure.

The two principal methods of catching pilchards were by seining and drift-net fishing. In drift-net fishing, the fishermen could be said to be self-employed, one man providing the boat and others a portion of the nets, each man receiving a proportionate share of the catch. Seine fishing, however, was in the hands of fish merchants and dealers. Local landowners would often have shares as an investment. Substantial capital was needed for the enterprise as two or three boats and large nets were necessary, as were pressing equipment, cellars, salt and barrels. Fishermen were employed for a fixed wage. The merchant financing the fishery in his turn sold on the pilchards to bigger merchants, who organised the export of the fish. Falmouth, Penryn and Fowey had emerged by the early eighteenth century as Cornish ports from which pilchards were shipped abroad.

Seine Fishing

Pilchards approached the land in shoals during the late summer. Lookouts, called *huers*, signalled the arrival of a pilchard shoal with cries of *hevva, hevva* through a long tin trumpet, and by hand signals. Hand signals, a type of semaphore, were then used to give directions to the fishermen in the seine boats. Where more convenient this operation was

directed from a boat known as a *lurker*. The main seine boat, about 30 - 40 feet in length, was a low boat, broad in the beam and sharp in the bows. Manned by six to eight oarsmen, this boat carried the seine net, a long, fine mesh net with cork floats in which the shoal of fish, or as much of it as possible, was enclosed. A second boat, known as a *volyer*, carried the tuck net (used to take fish from the seine net) and also equipment for mooring the seine. Once the fish were enclosed, the catch was hauled into shallow waters where the seine could be anchored. The fish were then dredged from the seine with the smaller tuck net and scooped from this into baskets. These were transferred to small boats and the fish taken ashore for processing. If necessary the fish could be kept in their net enclosure for a few days, being removed as required for salting and pressing. The seine was believed to be the best way to catch pilchard; legislation prohibited pilchard and mackerel driving-boats (luggers) from breaking up the shoals of fish before they reached the shore. They were not permitted to fish within prescribed limits, a law which led to constant disputes between the seiners and drifters, and which was not always observed.

Drift fishing

The main mackerel fishing season lasted from March to the beginning of the pilchard season in July. During the nineteenth century, some of the bigger luggers sailed to Ireland in July and August to take part in

the summer herring fishery. Some boats would then continue to Scotland, go through the Caledonian Canal and down the East Coast following the herring shoals. They would then fish out of one of the East Coast ports, such as Whitby or Scarborough. These boats were away for several months. In the early years of the twentieth century shoals of herring were discovered off Plymouth, much more accessible and the fishermen could occasionally come home. The Plymouth herring season lasted from November to the middle of February, then it would be time to fit out the boats again for the start of the mackerel season.

Line fishing was traditionally used for demersal, or bottom feeding, fish such as cod, haddock, ling, sole and turbot. The trawl began to replace hook-and-line in the eighteenth century. Trawlers had to be larger and stronger than drifters, with a more powerful sail plan. These were deep sea boats, able to ride out storms and powerful enough to tow the trawl. Steam powered fishing boats started to arrive from the east coast on the Cornish fishing grounds between 1860 and 1870. The Cornish showed some reluctance to change to steam. Coal had to be brought from South Wales and was expensive. When internal-combustion engines first became available in about 1910, boats at last had the power to go to sea and return without the frustration of being becalmed.

The inventory of John Tonkin of Newlyn (who died in 1692) gives the value of his 'fishing boate, netts and other seafaring craft for fishinge' as being worth £5.6s.0d and 'a small parcell of new and old salt, press poles and other necessaries for pressing pilchards' £3.15s.0d. His house and garden was valued at £10 in an estate valued at over £154.[12] John Tonkin was a comparatively wealthy working fisherman who owned his own equipment.

In 1870 the average cost for building a pilchard-driver, a half-decked boat, ready for sea was £120. A much larger, fully decked mackerel driver about £200 complete.[13] The cost of building a fairly substantial granite stone house would have been much the same. By this time, with seine fishing declining, the records in the late nineteenth century show a high proportion of fishermen were again owners of their boats.

Today, with hugely expensive beam trawlers operating out of Newlyn, costing an average of half a million pounds each, a considerable number of the boats are part of the largest privately owned fishing fleet in Europe, that of W. Stevenson & Sons. Shipwrights, engineers, blacksmiths, office, market and pier staff, are all part of the operation necessary to service such a large undertaking, together with a need for refrigerated transport and ice plant. At the present time Newlyn fish market handles about twenty million pounds worth of fish each year and the harbour shelters up to two hundred boats. In addition to the large beam trawlers there are Gill Netters, Long Liners, Crabbers and Hand Liners. From a small beginning, Newlyn has become one of the principal fishing ports in Britain.

The Tithe System

Over the centuries there have been problems and John Tonkin, the seventeenth century fisherman already mentioned, was one of thirty fishermen sued in 1680 by the owner of the Paul tithes, William Gwavas, for non-payment. The tithe system was originally a tax levied by the Church. Dating from the Middle Ages, when many churches were built, it was regarded as a necessary tax and, even if not liked, was paid without protest. By the late seventeenth century many tithes had been taken over by private landowners and did not go for Church use. With the exception of the seine owners who were often more prosperous businessmen, many fishermen were poor. They bitterly resented their tithes and for one-and-a-half centuries from 1669 when William Gwavas inherited Paul Rectory and the tithe there was strong opposition. In the 1680 case he won the day, as he did four years later in an action against six men, including two merchants, Nicholas Boson and Nowell Tonkin. For some years tithes were paid, but there was a new crisis in 1725 when a case was brought by William Gwavas against one hundred and eighteen fishermen. By this time there was open revolt but the courts again decided for William Gwavas. The issue continued on a troubled path until 1830, with the fishermen paying only when they had no choice. On Christmas Eve of that year an attempt was made by a bailiff to serve writs on defaulters at Mousehole. It had been a poor drift-net season and times were hard. He was mobbed by the women of the village and then, as he retreated, battered and bruised, by the women of Newlyn. His pistols had been taken from him and cast into the sea. Prosecutions seemed imminent but the tithe-owners had been sufficiently intimidated and fish tithes were never collected again.

William Williams

In the archives of the Morrab Library at Penzance, there yet survives the journal of a fisherman. Living in Newlyn in the late 18th and early 19th centuries, William Williams died there in 1838. Each page is carefully headed *Remarkable Occurencies or Principal Events* but he is mainly concerned with ships and the sea. Almost every entry carefully records the wind direction and state of the weather. William started his journal in 1771 by making some entries about past events, the first of these being the burning of the village by the Spaniards in 1595. This was taken from the account written by Richard Carew, indicating William's familiarity with his *Survey of Cornwall*. He also records two very bad storms in October and November of 1738, which broke down part of Newlyn Quay. From 1771 until 1836 there are regular entries, although sometimes only two or three a year.

William was keeping his journal during the Napoleonic Wars, but there is no mention of Trafalgar or Waterloo. The comings and goings of naval ships in the Bay are recorded and, occasionally, accounts of distant battles. There are references to French and Spanish prizes anchored in Gwavas Lake, many references to wrecks, and to ships of war. The second of the extracts quoted below could refer to troops returning from the American War of Independence (1775-83):

> Nov. 30 1780. His Magjesty's cutter the Pilate being chased by a supposed French fricket [frigate] or large privateer ran ashore or aground in Porthcurnowe sand near the Lands End but was got off again with little or no damage and anchored in Gwavas Lake. Wind at ENE. Decr.4th. Wind abt ESE sailed ye cutter.
>
> 1784. January ye Eleventh. Wind at East. Three ships of abt 300 tons each; transports with troops on board. From New York. Anchored in Gwavas Lake.
>
> 1803. Decbr ye 23. Come in & anchor'd in Gwavas Lake (wind abt SSW) His Magjesty's ship the Plantagenent of 74 guns from Ushant in the fleet with Admiral Cornwalis[14] Admiral of ye Blue.
> Dec.28. Wind at WSW saild his Magjesty's ship, Plantagenet.
>
> Jany 26 1809. Wind at WSW a strong gale. Reports in circulation of a brig sloop of war lost upon the Manacles and only one man saved and likewise of a transport lost near the Blackhead with a hundred soldiers on board only seven men saved. Also of a vesel wreaked in Belurian & all the men drowned.[15]

The start of the mackerel and pilchard seining seasons are faithfully recorded. Although boats started going to Ireland for the herring fishery in 1826, this is not mentioned.

> 1802. Mar ye 1. on Monday 30 boats went a mackral droving the first of the year, one boat had 1600 of mackral, another 600, & the rest very little. Sold at 2 guineas a Hundred.

July 25 1803. Seyners time commenced for 8 weeks.

Sometimes wrecks brought rewards in the form of salvage:

> 1782. Aug 13th. At night wind about SW a rich laden ship of Venice from Marselias [Marseilles] bound to Ostend struck upon ye Crim rock near ye Islands of Scilly & was entirely lost or wrecked and two of ye ships company drowned in ye forecastle.
> 1782. Aug 19. Sundry sorts of Merchandize goods found in ye offing as oil, brandy, soap, wine & other valueable goods by Mounts Bay men. Wind at SSW.
> 1782. Aug.20. More goods found brandy, soap, etc. abt two leagues from ye Lands End. Wind about SW.

On the following day there is a detailed account of a trip he and a fellow fisherman, John Tonkings, made in the latter's boat to search for salvage. It sounded a fairly hazardous journey and it only yielded 'a chest with abt 30 small cakes of Castle Soap.'

The *Remarkable Occurencies* too were mainly concerned with the elements:

> 1811 This year about the middle of Sept. a bright Comet made his appearance in the Heaven; bearing about NE to N and continued inclining westward, till the end of the year or the beginning of 1812 when it disappeared in the NW or WNW.

> 1813 Jan ye 8. A large fish brought in to Newlyn. Called a Basking shark which yealded a hundred and eighty gallons of oil which sold for 3, 6 and 4d pr gallon.

John Wesley visited Newlyn on fourteen occasions between 1747 and 1789, but there is no mention of him in William William's Journal. We can, however, suppose that William attended Paul Church: a letter bound into the book, addressed to a friend, gives instructions about the payment of debts should he be lost at sea, any remaining money to be disposed of according to the discretion of the Revd Mr Gurney, then vicar of Paul. The letter is dated Saturday, 11th April 1818. March of that year had been particularly stormy and on the date in question the wind was at NNW, a strong gale with showers of snow or sleet.

That William Williams was literate is in itself remarkable. There is no mention of family but he has left us a legacy in his journal, which gives a vivid picture of the life and interests of a fisherman in late eighteenth and early nineteenth century Newlyn.

Religious life in Newlyn

Until 1828 in Britain the principle still existed of an Established Church, to which everyone belonged and had to support, notably through paying tithes. After 1689, you could worship away from the Church, but if you did so you lost your civil rights. You could not hold any public office or go to the University without affirming the beliefs and following the practices of the Church of England. In 1828 Parliament repealed the 17th century Test and Corporation Acts, thereby giving full citizenship to the Protestant nonconformists. In the following year the Roman Catholics, who had only been given freedom to worship as recently as 1791, were also granted full liberty.

In the early 19th century Cornwall did not have its own bishop but was part of the diocese of Exeter. The see of Truro was founded in 1876. Compared with other counties, notably with Devon, the Church of England had few parishes: at the beginning of the century Devon had 463 parishes and Cornwall 212.[16] That is not to say that there were the same number of clergymen; pluralism and non-residence affected both counties. The 1830s and '40s saw the creation of new ecclesiastical parishes, thirty-three in Cornwall of which Newlyn was one. Large parishes and remoteness from Exeter may have made the Church of England structurally weak in Cornwall and contributed to the rapid growth in nonconformity in the late 18th to the mid-19th centuries. The rise was spectacular, particularly through the Wesleyan Methodist denominations.

John Wesley, the founder of Methodism, was born in 1703 and ordained in the Church of England, as was his younger brother, Charles. As young men at Oxford they had come together with a few others to practice a life of self-discipline, regular devotion and active witness. According to John Wesley, their basic principles involved 'living according to the method laid down in the Bible', a statement

that gave rise to the name by which they were then known, the Oxford Methodists. Initially no new theology was involved, no break with the Church or revolt against tradition. Later Methodism was to take many shapes and forms, but essentially it started as a simpler form of worship in which ministers and lay people worked in partnership, living according to bible principles and with a belief in a close personal relationship with God. The Wesleys, and the preachers who followed their teaching, mainly spoke in the open air, as most parish clergy closed their pulpits against them, alarmed by their evangelistic zeal and the fear that frequent Methodist revivals would weaken the Church of England. Methodism was at first an evangelical movement within the Church of England, becoming a separate body in 1795. Often John Wesley and the other preachers were jeered at, shouted down, stoned and attacked by the people of the places they visited, but gradually Methodist chapels were built, although the first chapel in Newlyn was not built until ninety years after John Wesley's death.

John Wesley visited Cornwall thirty-two times and came to Newlyn on fourteen occasions, the last just two years before his death in 1791. On the 12th July 1747, his first visit, he wrote in his journal:

> At five I walked to a rising ground, near the seashore, where there was a smooth white sand to stand on. An immense multitude of people was gathered together, but their voice was as the roaring of the sea. I began to speak, and the noise died away.

He wrote that some poor wretches of Penzance caused a disturbance but he was helped by some of the Newlyn men. The next year he described the Newlyn congregation as:

> a rude, gaping, staring rabble-rout, some or other of whom were throwing dirt or stones continually. But before I had done all were quiet and still, and some looked as if they felt what was spoken.[17]

When he came in 1751 he notes that the bulk of his open-air congregation stood quite still despite a storm of rain and hail. The people became very strong in their faith and very active in attending services and class meetings. Traditionally Methodism was strong in fishing and mining communities; in villages such as Newlyn attendance at Methodist services was far in excess of that of the Church of England.

In 1851 a census of attendance at religious worship was taken. This was the only census of its kind taken by the state, so no figures are available for comparison. On the 30th March 1851 the returns show that 66.33% (2073 persons) of the population of the parish of Newlyn attended a place of worship, above the national average. Of these 40.18% attended the Wesleyan Church and 34.24% were Primitive Methodists, giving a total Methodist percentage of 74.42% (1543 persons). A further 13.02% of the population were Independents and 12.54% (260 persons) attended the Church of England services held in a 'Licensed Room' formerly used for the purpose of Divine Worship by a congregation of Protestant Dissenters as an Anglican church was still to be erected.[18]

At the present time Newlyn has two Methodist churches: Trinity Methodist Church opened in 1832 and the Centenary Chapel, built in 1927 to replace an earlier chapel, the Ebenezer Primitive Methodist Chapel, which had opened in Boase Street in 1835. Trinity was a Wesleyan Methodist Church when built, but in 1932 all churches within the Methodist movement came together to form the United Methodist Church. The Primitive Methodists had broken away from the Wesleyans early in the nineteenth century when they adopted Camp Meetings, an American form of evangelism condemned by the Wesleyan Conference. They were less inhibited in their worship than the Wesleyans, who followed a more formal pattern of service.

In his book *Newlyn Towners, Fishermen and Methodists - 1800-1978 An Outline History* Ben Batten describes a week in the life of the Ebenezer Chapel in the second half of the 19th century. It graphically shows the extent to which village life centred on its chapels and churches at that time:

> At Ebenezer Chapel the spiritual life was rarely less than vital, whatever the material circumstances of its members; for these the chapel was the centre and main interest of their lives. Primarily of course it was their place of worship, where they offered praises to God in company with those of like persuasion, and they worshipped as families. It is no exaggeration to say that for most of them the Chapel in all its aspects was the equivalent, in modern terms, of a religious sanctuary, a social club, a youth club and a choral society all gathered at various times

Trinity Methodist Church 'Band of Hope' banner.

under one roof. Sunday services were very well attended indeed and it is a truism to point out that there were barely any other attractions to affect attendance; the evening meeting tended to be considered more important, and was better attended. Before the morning service at 10.45 men's classes met, and, except during the winter months, open air meetings preceded the evening service. The latter was usually followed by a prayer-meeting, also well attended. The service started at 6 pm, there were always five hymns, sermons lasted normally from 25 minutes to 40 minutes, and so those who stayed to the 'after-meeting' would be in the chapel for two hours or so, and found this no hindrance or hardship. The large Sunday School met at 2.30 pm and lasted an hour, scholars' ages ranged from very young children to adolescents of 16 years or more. It is clear from the above details that an active member or Sunday School teacher would spend the greater part of the day in chapel activities.

Ebenezer was used regularly on weeknights, only Thursday not being a fixed evening. The Monday evening women's Class, a very large group, met at the end of a hard day at the wash-tray, and in that period when leisure time was far more limited for women like these, with large families and a never-ending series of domestic chores, the class meeting must have been a blessed hour of peace and refreshment of spirit. On Tuesday the weeknight preaching service was held (and this was on the chapel calendar for many years), on Wednesday the Young Women's Class met. Choir practice each week took place on Tuesday at 8 pm, or when convenient. There was always great keenness to join the choir, as it was considered an honour, and attendance at practices was most regular.

The Christian Endeavour was always a very flourishing and active organisation, and many chapel members bore the C.E. badge on their lapels. The Junior C.E. met at 6.30 pm on Fridays, and the seniors followed. Many budding local preachers and speakers gained their initial confidence in public speaking by delivering a 'topic', or written paper, at the junior session.

Preparation for the Lord's Day meant for many an almost obligatory attendance at the Saturday night prayer meeting, when prayer, exhortation and testimony were uttered, interspersed with hymns and choruses spontaneously sung. The Chapel Trustees sometimes met on Saturday evening, that being the most convenient time, for none would be out fishing then. A society leader, or class leader or Sunday-school official could well be involved in chapel affairs for the greater part of his or her leisure hours.

Gala days were big events for the children. The Band of Hope gala was held on Whit Monday. Accompanied by bands and carrying the Band of Hope banner a procession, mainly of children, wended its way through the streets of Newlyn and up through the Coombe to the grounds of Trereife House. Then followed races and games, stalls to be patronised and large saffron 'School treat' buns. Long discontinued, such days were big social events in the year. The Band of Hope is now disbanded but both chapels still have their banners with pictorial representations of the evil of Drink. The splendid Ebenezer banner was even painted by the Newlyn School artist, Frank Bramley.

Newlyn was part of Paul Parish until 1848 and people wishing to attend the Church of England services went to Paul Church, or if they lived at Tolcarne on the Penzance side of the Newlyn river, to Penzance or Madron. There is no clear evidence of the existence of an earlier Chapel-of-Ease at Newlyn. In 1848, because of the growth in population, the new ecclesiastical parish was formed out of parts of Madron and Paul parishes but the church of Newlyn St. Peter, dedicated to the patron saint of fishermen, did not have its opening service until the 6th February 1866.

The church was built mainly through the efforts of the third vicar, the Reverend John Pope Vibert, a Penzance man, enthusiastic, energetic and dedicated. Appointed in 1856, he soon started to raise funds to build a church, but it was to be ten years before he had the satisfaction of seeing it completed. The land was given by the Le Grice family of Trereife and the estimate for building the church was £2,000. It is in the Early English style and built of local walling stone with dressings of granite from the nearby Lamorna quarry. There was insufficient money to complete the building and the north aisle was not added until 1886. A planned 70ft spire was never built, but a more modest turret eventually completed the building. Near the porch entrance is an ancient cross head, mounted on a modern shaft. The cross is in the form of a short, thick Latin cross, with a roughly sculpted Christ figure on the front.

A Famous Son of Newlyn

William Lovett, the nineteenth century Social Reformer, was born on May 8th, 1800 in Church Lane, Newlyn, in one of the thatched cottages which once stood where the Centenary Methodist Chapel now stands. He was arguably Newlyn's most famous son, rating nearly five columns in the *Dictionary of National Biography*. His father, captain of a small trading vessel, was drowned at sea before his birth and he was brought up by the family of his mother, Keziah Green. From 1844 until 1874, three years before his death, William Lovett kept a record of his life and it is this autobiography which gives details of his early life in Newlyn, and in Sancreed, where he spent some time with his great-grandmother. It was she, he relates, who taught him to read. At an early age he went to dame school and then to the boys school in Newlyn, transferring to the school at Paul. His mother was a strict Methodist and on Sundays, between attendances at chapel, he read texts, prayers and portions of scripture. He was fond of reading from boyhood, but there were few books available to him. From school he was apprenticed to a rope-maker. In his spare time, having a natural aptitude for handling tools and with access to a carpenter's shop, he acquired proficiency in carpentry. It was here that it was suggested to him that he should try his fortune in London. He had insufficient money for the journey. To raise it he later wrote:

> ....with a few shillings I had raised I purchased some mahogany veneers and other requisites for making a lady's workbox, with secret drawers, together with a pair of tea-caddies. These I got up in the best style I was master of, and being fortunate enough to dispose of them, together with two or three little trinkets I had by me, I increased by these means my stock of money to about fifty shillings. Having got so much towards my voyage, I commenced another work-box which, when I set out for London, the captain of a small trading vessel agreed to take as part payment for my passage money.

He left home on the 23rd June, 1821 and was only to return to Newlyn twice, in 1840 and 1852, on the last occasion to see his mother before she died.

Eventually Lovett, was successful in obtaining work as a cabinet maker in London and joined the Cabinet Makers' Society, of which he subsequently became President. He found opportunities to improve his education, joining various literary, scientific and political associations. Here he met others who shared his ambition of improving social conditions. In 1826 he married a lady's maid called Mary, whom he met at Marylebone Church, where he had gone to hear a special preacher.

For William Lovett education and temperance were the path to social reform. He was a moderate who set out to persuade others by reason rather than by physical force. In 1831 he refused to serve in the Militia, arguing that he had no vote in selecting Parliament and therefore should not be compelled to take up arms to protect the rights and property of others, while his rights were not protected. For this he was fined and goods seized from him in payment. At this time only some 800,000 people out of a population of 25 million had the right to vote. Even after the changes established by the Reform Act of 1832, only one man out of every seven in the country had this right. In the same year Lovett exposed the conditions under which the poor were herded in the workhouses, so familiar in Dickens.

By now a leader among Working Mens Associations, William Lovett was involved in the battle for political reform, drafting the demands of *The People's Charter*. In 1839, as Secretary of the General Convention of the Industrial Classes, he organised a meeting in Birmingham. The meeting was prohibited, whereupon the Convention passed three resolutions of protest at this interference with the liberties of the people, which they then had printed. The resolutions had been drawn up and signed by Lovett. He was arrested and sentenced to a year's imprisonment for publishing 'a seditious libel'. While in prison he wrote a book *Chartism, or a New Organisation of the People.*

From now on much of his energy concentrated on improving education, starting Free Schools which he managed, and in which he taught. He also wrote text books, often studying a subject himself in order to do so. He wrote:

> I regard as *true religion* that teaching which is based on the great and broad principles of human brotherhood, of reciprocal Christian duty, of mental freedom in the pursuit of truth, of love and kindness for the whole human family, and of the necessity for each and all of us doing all in our power for the mental, moral and physical education of our race.[19]

William Lovett died on August 8th, 1877 and is commemerated in Newlyn by a tablet in Fore Street which reads:

> To the honoured memory of William Lovett. As a National Leader in Social Reform he suffered imprisonment for advocating liberties which we now enjoy. 1800-1877.

Cholera Outbreak

There are four churchyards in Paul. One of them is a pleasant field with gravestones around the walls, but in three terrible months in 1832, eighty-eight victims of cholera, mainly from Newlyn, were buried there. An outbreak of cholera had been reported in Sunderland in 1831; it quickly spread to Newcastle. The disease reached London in February, 1832 and by then it was certain that the country was dealing with a major epidemic. An Order in Council was made stating that all persons dying of the disease should be buried within twenty-four hours in land set aside for that purpose and enclosed.

By June of 1832, the cholera had reached Plymouth and it was clear that Cornwall would not escape. By the end of the first week in August, cholera had appeared in Newlyn.[20] The Newlyn outbreak was alleged to have been brought in by fishermen returning from Ireland; Thomas Gibbard, a fisherman recently returned from that country, was thought to have brought the disease back with him; he was buried on 30th July.[21] By the end of August, cases were being reported from all over Cornwall.

When cholera first appeared in Newlyn, the people of Mousehole enforced a local quarantine to prevent all communication with the infected places, thus prohibiting the inhabitants of Newlyn from passing through their streets. When, however, the disease seemed to be diminishing, they removed their quarantine system; but the people of Newlyn, who had resented this unneighbourly act, retaliated by prohibiting the passage of Mousehole folk through Newlyn. This was an entirely different matter, for few Newlyners had occasion to go to Mousehole, but the route from Mousehole to the market town of Penzance lay through Newlyn. The outcome was a battle in Newlyn when the Mousehole villagers were put to flight. Magistrates were called to the scene and with the aid of a body of constables managed to arrest one of the ringleaders of the disturbance, who was bound over to keep the peace.[22]

Street-an-Nowan and Tolcarne

As the fishing village of Newlyn expanded on the high ground surrounding the medieval harbour, so at the bottom of the hill on the level ground surrounding the Newlyn river another community was developing. With running water to provide power this was to be of an industrial nature. Although separated physically at high tide, the beach provided the linking factor, for it was here that many of the day-to-day activities of the two communities were centred. From early times the small harbour enclosed by the fifteenth century quay had failed to provide adequate shelter for the growing Newlyn fishing fleet; this mainly anchored off shore, relying for shelter on the headland, which offered little protection from south and south easterly gales. Fish were transferred to the shore in small boats and it was on the beach that fish sales took place. To the beach also, the fishermen went to repair and refit their boats and spread sails and nets to dry. Fish baskets and boxes would be washed in the Newlyn river that flowed down the Coombe, dividing Street-an-Nowan and Tolcarne.

Tolcarne Mill

Until 1848, when the Ecclesiastical parish of Newlyn was formed, Tolcarne was part of the parish of Madron and of the Manor of Alverton. The manorial mill of Alverton was at Tolcarne on the Madron side of the Newlyn river (see map page 32) and here the Lord of the Manor exercised his right to compel all inhabitants within the Manor to grind their corn at his mill and not elsewhere. At some time in the sixteenth century the mill (with its privileges) had been granted by the Crown, who then held the Manor, to a branch of the Godolphin family living at Trewarveneth in Newlyn. It thereafter remained in separate ownership from the rest of the Manor.[23] Rival millers and bakers resented this obligation to use the Tolcarne Mill. Under the leadership of the then Mayor of Penzance, they set up other mills. A series of successful court actions, brought by the Godolphin family, ensued between 1623 and 1639. For a while the Penzance Corporation and townspeople accepted defeat and there was little trouble while the mill remained the property of Colonel William Godolphin of Trewarveneth. He was for some years the Recorder of Penzance and a good friend to that town. He died without issue, leaving the mill to his wife, his nephew, William Nicholls of Trereife, and two great nieces. In about 1650 a Nicholls had married the co-heiress of the Godolphins of Trewarveneth. William Nicholl's share passed to his son, John Nicholls, a successful

Middle Temple barrister. In about 1710, determined to enforce his rights, he brought a case against the Corporation of Penzance and two millers. There were sixty-eight individual defendants. Finally in 1714, on legal advice, they all submitted to judgement in favour of Nicholls, confirming the obligation to grind at Tolcarne. John Nicholls died the same year; the mill at Tolcarne remained the property of his descendants and their successors, the Le Grice family, for many years.

Tolcarne Mill was again to become the subject of litigation in 1883, when James Runnals, proprietor of Penlee Quarry, was the defendant in a suit at Chancery brought by Robert James, of Herbert Villa, Tolcarne, to restrain Mr. Runnals from working a stone crusher immediately behind the plaintiff's house. Tolcarne Mill was then being used to crush stone for road building. At that time, James Runnals was constructing the road bridge and new road leading to Penzance: the old Newlyn to Penzance road across the seafront had been washed away in a storm in 1880.

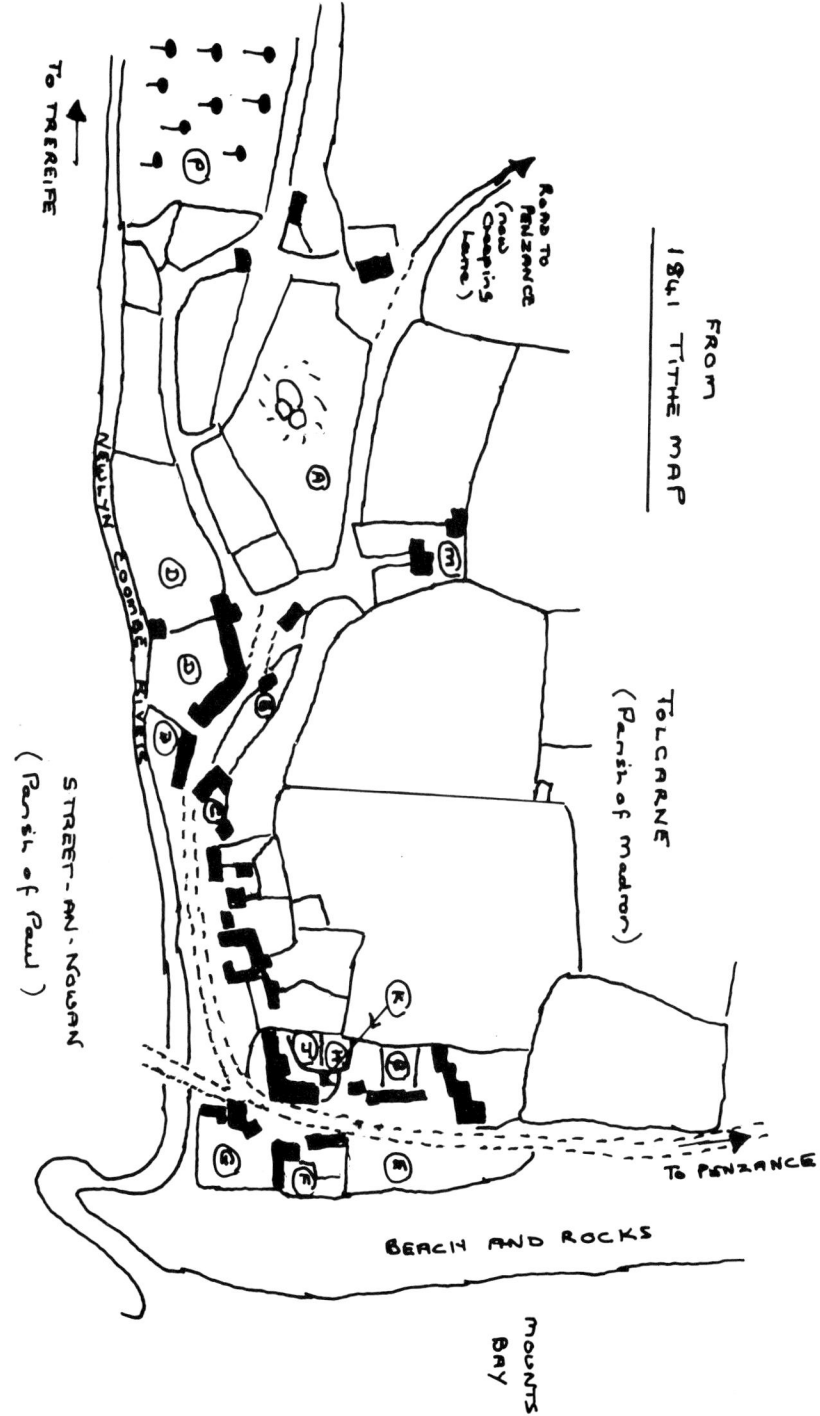

Trereife

Early records show that the Nicholls family were the owners of Newlyn Coombe down to and including Tolcarne foreshore. This included all the property shown on the section of the 1841 tithe map reproduced here, the farmland extending towards the Larrigan river at Penzance and back up the length of the Coombe to Trereife House. Parts of the house date back to the seventeenth century but the major part was built in the early 18th century by John Nicholls. Polsue wrote:

> One of the oldest seats in the parish is Trereife, *the town of the reeve*, the property and residence of Day Perry Le Grice, Esq. The estate belonged to the family of Nicholls from time immemorial, who also held the great tithes of the parish [Madron], which they inherited from the Flemings of Landithy, to whom they had been granted in the reign of Henry VIII. [24]

In 1590 William Nicholls had married Elizabeth Fleming of Landithy, whose dowry was the lay tithe of Madron. The estate passed down through the Nicholls family to William John Godolphin Nicholls who died at an early age in 1815. During 1808 the Trereife Estate had been disentailed and his mother became the absolute owner of Trereife House. Widowed at an early age, she had married in 1799 the Rev. Charles Valentine Le Grice, who had come to Trereife as tutor to her son. In this marriage she had another son, Day Perry Le Grice, from whom the family now living at Trereife is descended. The Le Grice family, according to Polsue, were of great antiquity in the counties of Norfolk and Suffolk, having settled at Brockclist, near Yarmouth, as far back as 1420.

Tolcarne in 1841

The plan on the facing page is based on the map of Madron Parish made when a survey of England and Wales was carried out as an aid to reforming the tithe system.[25] All of the land shown was owned at that date by the Le Grice family of Trereife. The chart below gives the type of business carried on in the areas indicated and the name of the occupier, in most cases also the lessee.

A	Mount Prospect Field (Tolcarne Rock)	
B	Higher Tolcarne Mill	Henry Grylls/John Pollard
C	Lower Tolcarne Mill	Richard Frean
D	Cooperage, Brewery, Offices & Yard	Gurney, Downing & others
E	Rope Walk	Justinian Carter
F	Tolcarne Public House	John Adams
G	Smith's Shop	Jackeh Rowe
H	Smith's Shop	Thomas Cattran
J	Timber Yard	Abraham Chirgwin
K	Miller	John Burt
M	Farmhouse	Charles Ladner
P	Orchards	William Ladner

(Orchards lined the river bank stretching up the Coombe)

Q	Carpenter's Shop	William Peake & others

The present St. Peter's Church, Church Hall and the Meadery are built on the site of the brewery and cooperage. The building at the top of the steps at the back of the church, now called Tolcarne Farmhouse, was once part of the brewery complex. A description of the Newlyn Brewery exists in a newspaper advertisement of 1828, when it was offered for sale by the then owner, John Richards, who was retiring from the business 'having realised a large fortune therein.'

> The Brewery has two Vats of 63 Barrels each; two Malt Mills, (one worked by a water-wheel); is abundantly supplied with excellent Water, conducted through it, and has every other article and convenience requisite for carrying on an extensive Business, and for Brewing every day. Adjoining the Brewery are ample Granaries, Malthouses, a Cooper's Shop, Stabling, Cart-Houses and Offices, with a large Garden and an extensive plot of Ground, on which the Brewery or Buildings may be enlarged. [26]

John Richards was also the proprietor of several 'Freehold and Leasehold Inns or Ale Houses' in Penzance and neighbourhood which were also to be sold. Just four months later Messrs Gurney and Downing were informing the public that they had purchased the Brewery.

Across the river in Street-an-Nowan there was more industry; in Foundry Lane, the Mount's Bay Foundry operated for a number of years. It had ceased to be listed in trade directories by 1883. Part of the premises were used by Mr R. R. Bath when he established a business for importing ice direct from Norway in 1887. This was on the site of the present Ice Works. There was also an ice store in the Coombe, built in 1873 and today the site of the Pilchard Works. The ice was brought by cart from the Gulval Ice Works and the store, 50ft by 17ft, stored 600 tons of ice.[27]

Fish stores and basket makers, sail makers and shipwrights could all be found in Street-an-Nowan. Baskets were made for farming as well as the fishing industry, especially after the coming of the railway saw large quantities of early potatoes, broccoli and Spring flowers despatched during the season. Ships continued to be used as a means of transport. There was reputed to have been a saw-pit on the site of the present Fishermen's Mission. Cobblers, shoemakers, bakehouses, shops and inns would have added to the general bustle of activity. These small businesses were interspersed with cottages, many arranged in 'courts' rather than rows. By 1850 a few larger houses were beginning to appear, straggling up the hill above the Coombe.

It was at Vine Cottage in the Coombe that a voyage was planned that was to make sailing history. In 1854 a Newlyn lugger, converted into a sailing yacht, made the first recorded ocean voyage by a boat of this type to Australia. The *Mystery* (PE233) was built in Newlyn for mackerel driving, her overall length being just 36 feet. The voyage was possibly prompted by the difficult times in the Cornish tin mining industry, aided by a spirit of adventure. Newlyn families had already emigrated to Australia and letters 'home' were doubtless enthusiastic about the opportunities available. The crew of seven, captained by Richard Nicholls as navigator, left Newlyn on November 18th, 1854 and arrived in Melbourne one hundred and sixteen days later on March 14th, 1855. They had sailed through mountainous seas and at times hurricane force winds. A plaque on the wall of the Newlyn Mission to Deep Sea Fishermen commemorates the epic voyage. Of the seven man crew, five returned to Cornwall. The *Mystery* was sold in Melbourne.[28]

Mining

At the top of the river valley, at Stable Hobba on the Tolcarne side of the river, was the large Trereife Tin Smelting Works, this had been established before 1732 and closed in 1896. Peter Laws, in describing the system of refining tin, referred to the smelter 'belching forth black murky smoke' [29] In the 1880s the smelting works incorporated a steam-powered saw mill for the cooperage, the barrels being used to pack bar tin for transport by sea or rail. The Trereife works used the heraldic bird motif as a stamp on its ingots, ingots that were shipped from Penzance.

There was considerable mining activity in the area and there were at least two mines in Newlyn itself, discounting the spectacular Wherry mine, stretching out to sea, which lay within the boundaries of Penzance. One of these mines was West Tolvedden on the site later occupied by the Penlee Quarry. Here a shaft known as Wheal Henry was sunk in 1828, on a copper lode. Further mining took place in 1852-4 and in 1858 a new Company was formed, being wound up in 1863. At the top of Paul Hill, at a site marked today by Adit Lane, was Wheal Elizabeth, generally known as Wheal Betsy. In 1851 the Mining Journal reported that this mine had 'a large engine house recently erected and other requisite buildings in progress towards developing the underground riches supposed to run through this extensive sett.' The mine did not last long, closing in 1853. It was a short lived venture.

In 1957, an advertisement appeared in the *Cornishman* newspaper offering land for sale. Lot 2 included 'the Freehold Fields known as Wheal Bal' giving an OS Map location in the Faugan area of Newlyn, as depicted in the sketch below.[30] This prompted Arthur J. Saundry of Penzance to write to the historian, Hamilton Jenkin:

> ...On Sunday evening I visited this area...approaching from the Chyenhal Moor side, which is probably the best way. There is a shaft in the position marked, and about 200 yards from Higher Faugan House. Shaft is surrounded by Cornish Hedge about seven feet high, topped by concrete posts with stout galvanised wire, and tram rails---if these came from the working of the mine they are lasting very well. The shaft top is much overgrown, but the shaft is open. There is no spoil or burrows, although there is much overgrown area adjacent to field 1086, which could well conceal other workings.
> The mine was probably worked by way of the lane running to Tredavoe. This has now degenerated into an overgrown footpath. I could find no trace of other shafts, but if land were developed for agriculture after the closing of the mine these might have been sollared over. The mine might also have some connection with Adit Lane....this is not so far away.[31]

It is this last sentence which suggests that possibly this was part of Wheal Betsy, or was it a third mine? There is no record of a reply to the letter other than a note that it was acknowledged on the 8th August 1957.

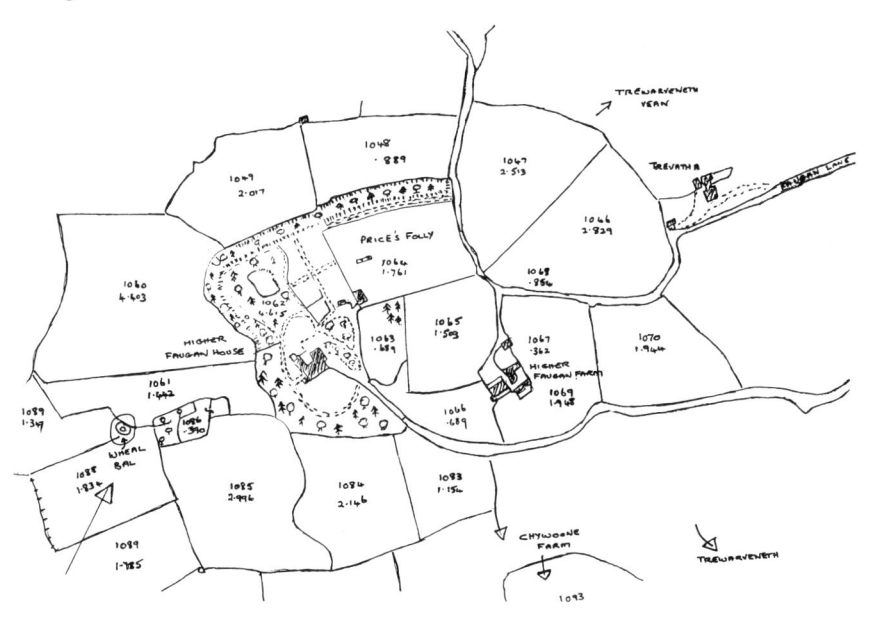

Newlyn School Artists

The artists who were to become known as the 'Newlyn School' discovered the village in the early 1880s. Approaching from Penzance they would first reach industrial Tolcarne, before crossing the bridge into Street-an-Nowan. Here, in the years to come they were to find subjects really worthy of painting. Initially, however, their interest would have centred on activities on the beach, the small harbour and the houses surrounding it. Here many of them would find lodgings and studios, and later those that stayed would build houses, high on the hill overlooking Mounts Bay. The twenty years from 1880 to 1900 established world reputations for many of these artists; these years also saw considerable development in Newlyn - linking its several parts into the busy fishing port it is today.

There were artists living and working in the area before the first of the recognised 'Newlyn' artists arrived. Henry Martin had lived in Newlyn since at least 1871, when his name appeared on the Census Return for that year, as it did in 1881. He moved away after that, but retained some links with the area; in 1889 he was exhibiting at the West Cornwall Art Union Exhibition in Penzance.[32] There were others, attracted by the varied scenery and quality of light found in West Penwith.

The artists who arrived in the 1880s were distinguished by their youth, and by their addiction to the 'en plein air' school of painting. Some would have studied with, or been influenced by, Jules Bastien-Lepage (1848-1884), a French painter, mainly of rustic scenes, who painted largely from nature. He was an important influence on many

British painters of the period, enthusing them with his belief that it was important to paint realist subjects in their natural setting. Lepage could be considered a social realist; however most of the Newlyn artists, while they felt it necessary to record life, did not seek to expose social conditions. The need to sell meant that their subjects must also be commercial. Contemporary accounts suggest that they did not want to paint in the classical style, or in that of the Pre-Raphaelites, such as Rossetti or Burne-Jones. It was a period of transition in British Art.

Among the first of the recognised 'Newlyn' artists to arrive was the Birmingham artist, Walter Langley. He had been in Newlyn prior to 1880 and returned in 1882 when he was given a commission for a year's work. He was joined by another Birmingham artist, Edwin Harris. Caroline Yates, who had studied at the Slade, was an early visitor; she married the painter Thomas Gotch at St. Peter's Church, Newlyn in 1881. Frank Bramley was yet another early arrival. In the issue of the *Cornishman* newspaper for September 4th, 1886 it was noted that there were now twenty-seven artists residing in Newlyn. Many of these did not settle in Newlyn: they came and went, spending part of the year painting elsewhere, perhaps in France or Holland. Their work has been documented and discussed in a number of books, some of which are listed in the bibliography (page 52).

By the late 1890s the artists had started to disperse, leaving behind a number who had settled in Newlyn. These included Stanhope Forbes and his wife, Elizabeth Armstrong; married in 1889, they were to set up their School of Painting in 1899. A new generation of painters then came to study in the village. Among the many artists painting in Newlyn at this time was a Cornishman, Harold Harvey (1874-1941). Born in Penzance from a long line of Cornish stock, he moved to Newlyn on his marriage and throughout his life painted local subjects. His interior scenes provide an insight into the life of the artist community at that time.

A number of the artists contributed to the life of the village in other ways and this led to the founding of the Newlyn Industrial Class in 1890. The fishing industry being an unreliable source of income, this venture aimed to provide employment during periods when bad weather and seasonal fluctuations in fishing brought enforced periods of inactivity. A local benefactor, T. B. Bolitho, provided some initial funding and the artists, notably J. D. Mackenzie, the expertise. After some early experiments, the class specialised in repoussé copperwork. This was not a field in which the artists themselves had skills and they were joined by a metal-beater, John Pearson, an established craftsman and founder member of the Guild of Handicraft. He appears to have worked with them for several years. The class produced a wide range of domestic and decorative items. The four decorative plaques on the facade of the Newlyn Art Gallery are a tribute to the work of the Industrial Class. They represent the four Elements: Earth, Air, Fire and Water. Classes in enamelling and silver work were held by the painter, Reginald Dick, whose wife also taught embroidery.

It was in Newlyn that the Crysede Silk Works were first established in 1920 by Alec Walker. Raw silk was bleached, dyed and hand-block printed in his designs. The silk was sold by the yard or made up into garments designed by his wife, Kay Walker. The first shop they opened was in Newlyn; this was followed by several other branches. The business moved to premises in St. Ives in 1926. All of these ventures provided employment for local people and added to the reputation of Newlyn as an artistic centre.

Newlyn Art Gallery

The Cornish philanthropist, John Passmore Edwards (1823-1911) paid for some seventy public buildings in England, including twenty in Cornwall. Among these was the Newlyn Art Gallery, given as a 'show place' for the artists and for the benefit of the public. Passmore Edwards laid the foundation stone in May 1895, using a trowel of 'exquisite design' in beaten metal - a mixture of tin and copper - a sample of the repoussé work produced by the Newlyn Industrial Class.[33] The land on which the gallery was built was given by Charles Le Grice of Trereife.

Today the gallery, as originally intended, remains a show place for contemporary artists. It also fulfils its commitment to work 'for the public good', through educational projects in schools, art clubs and a lecture series. A permanent collection of the work of the original 'Newlyn School' artists is held at the Penlee Art Gallery and Museum in Penzance. The Newlyn Society of Artists, established in 1895, still exists today.

A Time of Growth

By the mid nineteenth century, Newlyn had developed into a fishing port of note. The village was considered to have the finest mackerel and pilchard fishing fleet of any Cornish port. The existing quay, however, offered shelter to only a small number of boats and Gwavas Lake was an unsafe anchorage when strong easterly winds prevailed. Boats would then have to seek shelter in Penzance harbour. In 1795, petition had been made to Parliament for leave to bring in a Bill for a new pier at Newlyn. This was successfully opposed by Penzance, the town sending witnesses to London to give evidence against the bills.[34] Penzance had considerably improved its own harbour during the eighteenth century, and there were further major extensions to the piers in the early years of the nineteenth.

In 1865 *two* rival schemes were produced for building a new pier at Newlyn, one from local promotors, the Mount's Bay Harbour Company and the other from the Newlyn Pier and Harbour Company. The latter scheme won Parliamentary approval and a Provisional Order was made in 1866. Despite lack of progress, the Order was enforceable until 31st July, 1871, at which date the company successfully obtained additional powers and an extension of time. Again no actual work resulted, although in 1872 the Newlyn Pier and Harbour Company produced a revised harbour scheme which met with the approval of the fishermen.

Luckily, in 1874 the Revd W.S. Lach-Szyrma arrived in Newlyn as vicar of St. Peter's Church. From the start, he was active in the life of the village, reflected in newspaper reports of the day, parish and other records. The son of a University professor who had fled from Poland when revolution broke out in that country, Wladsyslaw Somerville Lach-Szyrma was born in Devonport in 1841. Growing up in Plymouth, he took an early interest in the fishing industry. The loss of fishermen, and of boats, was an all-too-common occurrence, leaving men without a livelihood and widows in poverty. A few years after the Revd Lach-Szyrma came to Newlyn, two boats, the *Primitive* of Mousehole and the *Malakoff* of Newlyn, were lost within a day of each other in 1879. This emphasised the need for some form of insurance; the Mount's Bay Fishing Boats' Mutual Insurance Club was set up, largely through the efforts of Lach-Szyrma, and it was registered as a Friendly Society. A few months later, in October 1880, a fully decked lugger, the *Jane*, was lost with all hands just one hundred yards from the shore, while making for Penzance harbour in a strong SSE gale.

These events led to the revival of proposals to build a large artificial harbour at Newlyn, the previous scheme having been dropped through lack of financial support. The money would have to be raised by voluntary fund raising efforts and from grants or loans. A committee was formed in 1882, with Lach-Szyrma as chairman. The foundation stone of the South Pier was laid on St Peter's Day, June 29th 1885 and the pier was ready for use at the end of the following year. The North Pier was started in 1888 and lengthened in 1893-94.

In the storms of 1880 the sea front had been badly damaged and the road leading along the shore from Tolcarne to Penzance was washed away. A New Road was constructed further inland, still known by that name today. Opened in 1883, it necessitated the construction of a road bridge, so there were now three bridges spanning the river at Tolcarne.

Opposite the new bridge, the road was continued in 1890 by cutting through to the top of Jack Lane. This stretch of road, Lower Chywoone Hill, is the one known locally as 'Bucca's Pass'. Constructing it involved demolishing a number of old cottages. In their place at the foot of the hill, and along the start of the Coombe, a number of large granite stores were built. Several are still fish stores, one now housing the premises of the shellfish merchants, W. Harvey & Sons, who also have extensive shell fish tanks adjacent to the South pier. On the hill, access now having been opened up, terraces of granite houses started to appear. Also in the 1890s, houses were built in the Tolcarne area on land previously farmed. Newlyn as it is today had started to emerge.

Newlyn 'town' and Street-an-Nowan were finally joined in 1908 by the construction of the Strand, the road replacing the broad stretch of foreshore where high tides had previously prevented direct access. The considerable quantities of stone needed to infill the site came from the Penlee Quarry, which in about 1890 had started up by the shore on the site of the earlier West Tolvedden mine. The stone worked, greenstone, was produced mainly for roadmaking. The

43

quarry was operated in the early years by James Runnals, who had previously worked two small quarries in the area. He owned a crushing-mill at Tolcarne and exported large quantities of crushed stone to ports in Wales. This quarry was to employ a large labour force in the first half of the present century, finally closing down in the 1990s.

In recent years, the increasing size of the fishing boats using Newlyn made it evident that there was a need for more deep water berths and improved landing facilities. The first phase of this development involved the construction of the Mary Williams Pier, dredging a deep water area and constructing a reclaimed area to provide working space and vehicle parking. This work was completed in 1980 and further developments, giving additional deep-water berthing and a new market building, were completed in 1988.

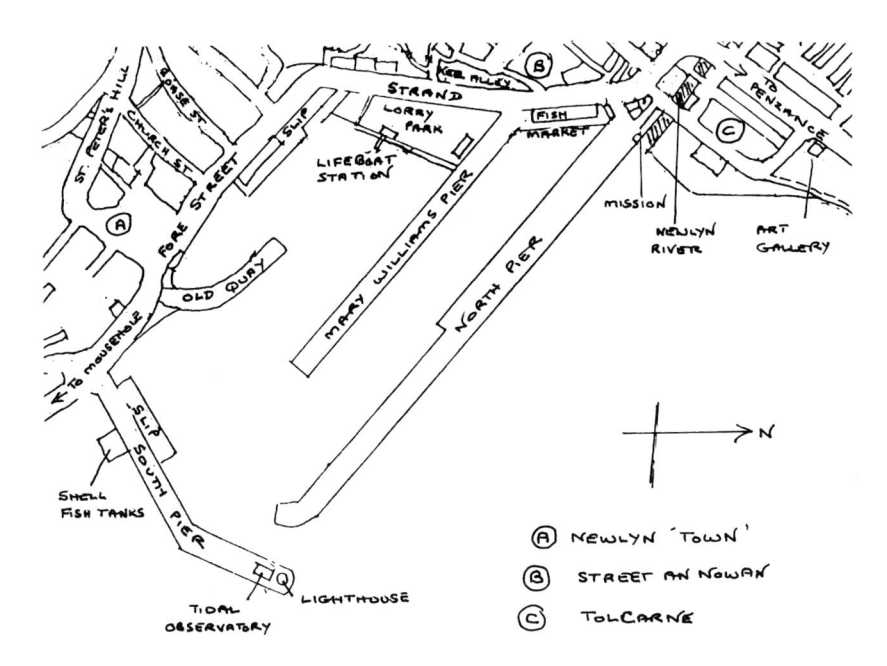

(A) NEWLYN 'TOWN'
(B) STREET AN NOWAN
(C) TOLCARNE

As deep-water berthing is available at all stages of the tide, the Penlee Lifeboat is now permanently stationed in Newlyn Harbour. The map above shows this development and also the position of the lighthouse and the Tidal Observatory on the end of the South pier. Here mean sea-level for the whole of the United Kingdom is determined. On Ordnance Survey maps heights are still measured from 'Mean Sea Level at Newlyn'.

The Ship Institute

The National Mission to Deep Sea Fishermen began its history of service to the fishing communities in 1881, working initially alongside the fishermen in the North Sea. From its Mission Ships, the Mission set about taking the message of Christ to the men on board the boats, providing practical comfort by means of medical aid, warm woollen clothing gifted by supporters, and cheap tobacco (which was not seen as the great social evil it is today). It was in 1887, following the publication of a book *Nor'ard of the Dogger* by Mather, recounting the early years of the Mission, that her Majesty Queen Victoria bestowed on the Mission its Royal patronage, a patronage continuing today.

In 1896 the Mission Council decided to send the *Euston*, a Mission ship, on an experimental trip to Cornish fishermen. The reception must have been favourable as, in 1899, the Mission ship *Ashton* visited Penzance under the command of Skipper Collett. By 1902, the reputation of the Mission, and the care and support it offered to the fishermen, was beginning to spread. The Cornish fishermen requested that the Mission should come down to Cornwall permanently and start a work in Newlyn. The request was sympathetically received and, in 1903, two members of the Mission Council were sent to Newlyn to find a suitable site.

On arrival they discovered that a Mrs Tonkin was already renting a house to fishermen on a short term basis. They were able to secure a fourteen year lease on the building, Skipper Collett, who had visited in 1896, was sent back to Newlyn to take charge of the newly opened 'Stanley Institute', the Mission building getting its name at the request of a benefactor, a Mrs Parker, who had given the Mission £500, a considerable sum at that time, to put up a 'Stanley Institute' at a site of their choice.

During 1904, it is recorded that Miss Nora Bolitho, from Trengwainton, was a regular visitor. She would spend time reading to the fishermen from papers and novels and she would write letters on their behalf. Already the building was becoming too small and she made a sum of money available to enlarge it and improve its facilities. By 1910, the work and ministry of the Mission had grown to such an extent that the Stanley Institute itself was now too small. Miss Nora Bolitho, always a valuable supporter of the Mission and its aims, offered to have a new building put up for the Mission in memory of her sister, Mary Foster, at a cost of over £4000, once again a considerable sum at that time.

It was on Saturday, 30th September 1911, that the doors of the building were 'quietly opened, a gift from Miss Nora Bolitho to the men of the fishing community'. From records and information available, it seems women were not allowed in the building (presumably with the exception of Miss Bolitho!) and boys had to be accompanied by their fathers. The name *Ship Institute* was officially approved. The copper galleon on the roof was made by Tom Batten and Francis Clemens of the Industrial Class.

With the outbreak of the 1914-18 war, the building was taken over as a base by the Royal Flying Corps. The Mission and its staff were then used to provide accommodation and welfare support to members of H.M. Patrol Vessels. The building was returned at the end of that War.[35] The Newlyn Mission is the base for the care and concern that is shown to all fishermen and their families throughout the whole of Cornwall. It also plays an important part in the life of Newlyn and has the respect of the local community.

The Newlyn Riots

Newlyn, as has earlier been seen, was strongly non-conformist. Not everyone in the village attended religious services on a Sunday, but the Sabbath was indeed kept holy. John Corin, in his book *Fishermen's Conflict*, wrote:

> ....some were more devout than others. James Henry Treloar Cliff, who became coxswain of the Porthoustock Lifeboat, records in his memoirs that in about 1892 he joined the Porthleven fishing boat *Emblem* for the Scottish herring fishery. They had a fair wind all the way up the Channel, but on coming abreast of Dover it was declared that as the morrow was Sunday they would put in and go to chapel. Cliff was a Church of England man and it was his only experience of missing a fair wind to go to chapel.[36]

In the nineteenth and early twentieth centuries, Mounts Bay boats did not go to sea on Sundays and hence did not land fish at the market on Mondays. The crews of the East Coast drifters which came to Newlyn for the mackerel season had no such scruples about Sunday fishing. Their boats were larger and more powerful than the Mounts Bay drifters; the crews were larger and, as they needed a greater financial return, so were their nets. All of these factors caused tension between the East Coast and Newlyn men, even before matters came to a head over Sunday fishing on Monday, 18th May, 1896.

On that morning, large crowds assembled to meet the East Coast boats coming in to land their fish. The boats were boarded and the mackerel thrown into the harbour. The protest seems to have been well planned as the fishermen of Mousehole, St. Ives and Porthleven responded to requests for help by preventing the East Coast boats from entering *their* harbours. Supporters from these villages arrived at Newlyn during that day and the next. Newlyn did not then come under the jurisdiction of the Penzance police, but under that of the County. There were only 219 police in the whole county at that time and it would be several hours before a large group of men could arrive.[37] In the meantime, the local Inspector of Police, with two of his constables and officials from H.M. Coastguard, attempted to intervene. A magistrate was called to attend, but it was decided that it was not necessary at this stage to read the official Riot Act.

For the rest of the day it was quieter, but the East Coast fleet was large and there were boats still at sea. On Tuesday 19th May several of these could be seen making for Penzance. Several hundred rioters set out to prevent them from landing their fish there. They were met by a small detachment of Penzance Borough police, supported by men who had responded to an appeal to enlist as Special Constables. They were backed up by other Penzance men, who appeared to be attracted only by the prospect of a fight with their rivals. The Newlyn men retreated.

Having decided that the situation might get worse, the Penzance authorities had asked for help. Shortly after 6 p.m., between three and four hundred men of the 2nd Berkshire Regiment arrived by special train at Penzance, where they were met by the Justices and the Chief Constable of Cornwall. They marched to temporary barracks at Wherrytown, on the outskirts of Newlyn. In the meantime a large number of Newlyn men, supported by others from Porthleven and St. Ives, set out for Penzance. Near the Lariggan river they met a crowd of Penzance men, augmented by a large number of Lowestoft fishermen. A serious fight ensued, despite the efforts of the police to control the situation. The soldiers were turned out and marched to Newlyn where they occupied the south pier. There were jeers but no serious incidents. Meanwhile a torpedo destroyer had arrived from Plymouth, shortly to be joined by three more destroyers. The fighting stopped; over the next few days, the authorities persuaded the East Coast boats to leave the port, so no further disturbances occurred. A detachment of the Berkshires remained in Newlyn for a time in case of further trouble. The presence of the soldiers and the warships had the desired effect, but was much resented by the Mounts Bay fishermen, who felt that they had had just cause for grievance.[38] After discussion, in which Bedford Bolitho, M.P. played an active role, the Lowestoft boats agreed that there should be no fishing on Saturday nights. The Newlyn boats continued not going to sea on Sundays. The subject of Sunday fishing remained a contentious issue, though not a major one, for many years.

The Journey of the Rosebud

In 1934 the Borough of Penzance was extended to take in Newlyn, Paul and Mousehole. The Council had the task of implementing the

Housing Acts. They decided to replace cottages at Newlyn with a new housing estate, the Gwavas Estate, to be built at the top of Chywoone Hill. Much of the housing to be replaced was admittedly sub-standard, but in their new modern homes the fishermen would not have storage space for their gear and all would be faced with climbing a 1 in 5 hill. The location of the new estate must have seemed remote to people used to living in close proximity with each other, their work, and the shops. Additionally, there was indignation that site-value only was to be paid to some of the house owners, many of whom had saved over generations to buy their homes. In the new houses on the Gwavas Estate, which were council owned, they would have to pay rent.

The Newlyn people reacted strongly and the Newlyn artists joined the cause. Penzance Council favoured a wholesale demolition approach and some of the artists' favourite subjects were doomed to disappear. It was decided to send a deputation to London to present a petition to the Minister of Housing. This was to be no ordinary deputation, for the petition was to be taken by a crew of Newlyn fishermen, in a Newlyn boat, up the Thames to Westminster Pier. The boat selected was the pilchard driver *Rosebud*, built in Newlyn in 1919. She left Newlyn at dawn on October 20th, 1937 for the 450-mile voyage to the Thames. Supporters travelled by train. The Rosebud arrived on October 22nd and attracted considerable public attention, but the result was not entirely satisfactory. Of the 157 properties in the Order, only 23 were excluded altogether.[39] A large number of properties were demolished but pressure on Penzance town council had some effect and the outbreak of war saved many properties. Many of these are now safe in a Conservation Area. A plaque on the wall of the Ship Institute commemorates the journey of the *Rosebud*, a very early example of modern style protests.

In the 1920s and 30s houses were built on the Lidden fields between Newlyn and Penzance; also, in post-war years, a municipal housing estate was built west of Penzance at Alverton. These developments have, in part, contributed to a physical link-up with Penzance. However, Newlyn maintains a strong sense of personal and separate identity and keeps its reputation as one of the most important fishing ports in the United Kingdom.

REFERENCES

1. In reality *streams* but locally the term *river* is used for relatively minor water flows.
2. P.A.S.Pool, *Place Names of West Penwith*,(2nd ed.1985)
3. J. Leland, *Itineraries,* (ed.T.Hearne 1769)
4. Confiteor unum baptisma in remissionem peccatorum, *I believe in one baptism for the remission of sins.*
S.M.C. of the English Dominican Congregation of Saint Catherine of Siena, *Once in Cornwall,* (Longmans, Green & Co. New York 1944), 19-20
5. P.L.Hull, *The Caption of Seisin of the Duchy of Cornwall*,136
6. G.C.Boase, *Collectanea Cornubiensa*, 1890 quoted by P.A.S.Pool in *History of Penzance,* (1974),20
7. J. Leland, *Itineraries,* (ed. T. Hearne 1769). *'Lytle socur of land water'* referring to the availability of the fresh water stream.
8. J. Norden, *Description of Cornwall* (1728),26
9. Quoted by W.S.Lach-Szyrma in *History of Penzance, S. Michael's Mount, S.Ives & the Lands End District* (Lake & Lake, Truro 1878),161
10. *Gwavas MS*, Morrab Library, Penzance.
11. W.S.Lach-Szyrma, *Newlyn and its Pier,* (F.Rodda, Penzance 1884)
12. James Whetter, *Old Cornwall,* Autumn 1966 Vol.VI. No.11
13. K. Harris, *Hevva! Cornish Fishing in the Days of Sail,* (Dyllansow Truran 1983)
14. Admiral the Hon. Sir William Cornwallis (1744-1819)
15. Manacles - rocks off St. Keverne in the Lizard.
 Belerion - The Lands-End, from *bol e rhin,* head of the promontory. Revd John Bannister 1871, *A Glossary of Cornish Names, Ancient & Modern.* William Williams could here be referring to the Lands End district or 'somewhere in Cornwall.'
16. Ed. Nicholas Orme, *Unity and Variety - A History of the Church in Devon and Cornwall,* (Univ. Exeter Press 1991),112
17. Ed. John Pearce, *The Wesleys in Cornwall,* (D. Bradford Barton Ltd. 1964)
18. Transcribed & edited by J.C.Probert, *Religious Census: West Cornwall and the Isles of Scilly,* (1998)
19. John J. Beckerlegge, *The Cornish Social Reformer - William Lovett of Newlyn,* (1948)
20. West Briton, 10.8.1832
21. West Briton, 17.8.1832
22. West Briton, 5.10.1832
John Rowe & C.T.Andrews, *Cholera in Cornwall,* (RIC Journal 1974. Vol.VII. Part 2)

23. P.A.S.Pool, *The History of Penzance*,35
24. Joseph Polsue, *Lake's Parochial History of Cornwall*, Vol.3,219
25. CRO Tithe Apportionment schedule (Madron)
26. West Briton & Cornwall Advertiser, 15.9.1828
27. Cornishman, 15.3.1883
28. Richard Kelynack Cocks, *The Mystery Voyage,* (1992)
29. Peter Laws, *The Industries of Penzance,* (Trevithick Soc.1978)
Stable Hobba, Eng. from *stable +hobba,* riding horse, (Pool, *Place Names of West Penwith)*
30. OS Map. Revision of 1936 edition. Sheet LXXIV 9
31. CRO X/565/18/2
32. Iris M.Green, *Artists at Home,* (1995),2
33. R.S.Best, *The Life and Good Works of John Passmore Edwards,* (Redruth 1981)
34. Peter Pool, *The History of Penzance*
35. From information provided by Len Scott, former Superintendent, Newlyn Mission.
36. John Corin, *Fishermen's Conflict,*(Tops'l Books 1988),10
37. *ibid*,68
38. Hutchings, *History of Cornwall County Police,* quoted in Pool, *History of Penzance.*
39. John Corin, *Fishermen's Conflict,*117

The Gaiety Cinema, opened in the early 1920s and much loved by 'Newlyners'. The building now houses the Newlyn Meadery.

BIBLIOGRAPHY

General

Joseph Polsue, *Lake's Parochial History of Cornwall,* (Truro 1867-73) (republished 1974 EP Publishing Ltd)
Colin M. Bristow, *Cornwall's Geology and Scenery,* (Cornish Hillside 1996)
K.C. Phillips (Ed) *The Cornish Journal of Charles Lee,* (Tabb House 1995)
John Pearce (Ed) *The Wesleys in Cornwall,* (D. Bradford Barton, 1964)
P.A.S. Pool, *The History of the Town and Borough of Penzance,* (1974)
Cyril Noall/Douglas Williams, *The Book of Penzance,* (Barracuda 1983)
O.J. Padel, *Dictionary of Cornish Place-Names,* (Alison Hodge 1988)
P.A.S. Pool, *Place Names of West Penwith* (Fed.OCS 1973)
Rev. W.S. Lach-Szyrma, *Short History of Penzance and Land's End,* (Truro1878)
Thomas Shaw, *History of Cornish Methodism,*(Bradford Barton 1967)

Books about Newlyn

Ben Batten, *Newlyn of Yesterday,* (1983)
Ben Batten, *Newlyn Boyhood*
Ben Batten, *School on the Hill - Paul School Board AD 1879 - Newlyn Infants School 1979,* (1979)
Ben Batten, *Newlyn Towners, Fisherman and Methodists 1800-1978* (1978)
Ben Batten, *Old Newlyn Speech,* (1984)
Ben Batten, *Walk Newlyn With Me,* (1981)
John Corin, *Fishermen's Conflict -The Story of Newlyn* (Tops'l Books 1988)
Alfred J. Kliskey, *Looking Back by a Newlyn Towner,* (1980)
Douglas Williams, *Around Newlyn, Mousehole and Paul,* (Bossiney 1988), [with many illustrations]
Rev. W.S. Lach-Szyrma, *Newlyn and its Pier,* (1896)

The Newlyn Artists

Caroline Fox, *Stanhope Forbes and the Newlyn School,* (David & Charles 1993)
Caroline Fox, *Artists of the Newlyn School 1880-1900,* (Exhib. Cat. 1979)
Caroline Fox, *Painting in Newlyn 1900-1930,*(Exhib. Cat. 1985)
Hazel Berriman, *Arts and Craft in Newlyn 1890-1930,* (Exhib. Cat.1986)
Iris M. Green, *Artists at Home- Newlyn 1870 -1900,* (1995)
Melissa Hardie (Ed), *100 Years in Newlyn - Diary of a Gallery,* (Patten Press & Newlyn Art Gallery 1995)
John Curnow Laity, *Newlyn Copper,* (Exhib. Cat. 1986)